Church Staff Evaluations:

A Guide to Performance Appraisals that Motivate, Develop and Reward Church Employees

Patricia Lotich

First Edition
Copyright © 2013 Patricia Lotich
Published by Create Space
ISBN-13: 978-1492355311
ISBN-10:1492355313

Contents

Foreword

"No great manager or leader ever fell from heaven, it's learned not inherited." Tom Northup

Working with church leaders has helped me recognize quite a few need help when managing employees. I decided to write this book because of the continued interest in this subject and the vulnerability that church leaders feel when asked to "assess" employee performance. I've had the privilege of overseeing church employees, and in speaking with other people who manage church staff, I truly understand the challenge that comes with trying to manage the day-to-day operations of a ministry and keeping employees focused on those things that are most important to church strategy.

I've worked with numerous church leaders who have or had the responsibility of managing church employees and dread the annual performance appraisal process. Partially, most church leaders dislike it because it's a time consuming process but, more commonly, because they don't have training and don't have the expertise to assess employee performance painlessly.

My hope is that this book will provide the tools to not only make the process easier but also the insights that can help to create a positive appraisal experience.

Anyone who works for a ministry understands the unique challenges that come with managing church employees. However, when employers manage with fairness and objectivity, the employees will feel more engaged with the church and go out of their way to create a positive experience for those people (employees, members and volunteers) they serve.

I ran across an interesting statistic that states, "An estimated 40 percent of all workers never receive performance evaluations. And for the 60 percent of the workers who do, most are poorly done...." That is a really scary thought and may explain a lot of the issues that organizations are dealing with today!

Christians are programmed to feel uncomfortable giving honest feedback. This is because they fear a perception of unchristian-like behavior. This fear creates an internal conflict that results in avoidance of those difficult conversations as well as a common perception that performance appraisals are a **worldly** exercise. And of course, the church leaders don't want the staff to view them as worldly – so we just pray that everything works out. Sometimes it does, but sometimes it doesn't.

Managing church employees really isn't any different from managing employees in other businesses with the exception of the spiritual component that's inherent in being a disciple of Christ. The natural side of running a church operation requires business principles that help manage the effects of the spiritual side of things. It's really all about training. Most things are improved with training – hence this book!

How to Use This Book

This book has six chapters. Each chapter progresses toward the ultimate goal of recognizing and rewarding employees for contributing to fulfilling the church's mission. This includes identifying employees who may not be performing at desired levels and then finally tying it all to the pay raise process.

Try to go through one chapter at a time and take some time to absorb the concepts and do the chapter assignment with your leadership team. This will allow you to progress from each chapter to the next seamlessly.

At the end I hope you will work with your team to develop a process to manage the people God sent to help you!

Book Overview

Chapter 1 – Managing Performance

In chapter 1 we lay some groundwork and introduce some theory about why managing performance is critical to achieving church objectives and what the specific advantages are to having a structured process to manage employee performance.

Chapter 2 – Setting Goals

Chapter 2 walks through the process of developing church goals and discusses why specific goals are so important to help move a church forward. We then walk through creating goals that are measurable and assigning accountability to someone to ensure he or she understands and completes the tasks.

Chapter 3 – Creating Performance Appraisal Form

In the chapter 3 we describe the process of developing a performance appraisal form that conforms to your church's values and employee responsibilities. This includes an example of a performance appraisal document that you can use as a template when you create your own form. A modifiable copy of this document is available at SmartChurchManagement.com/free-church-forms.

Chapter 4 – Performance Appraisal Process

In chapter 4 we get into the specific process of delivering a performance appraisal. This will take what we have so far full-spectrum – from writing goals, setting expectations, monitoring performance and putting it all together for that annual discussion. The goal of this chapter is to help the manager learn to create a positive experience for both the manager and employee.

Chapter 5 – Scoring and Attaching Performance Appraisals to Raises

In chapter 5 we take the performance appraisal forms that we created, score them, rank employees and learn how to tie the scores to raises. This will ultimately become a tool to objectively reward your best employees.

Chapter 6 – Employee Engagement and PA Process

Finally, in chapter 6 we discuss the importance of employee engagement and discover how the performance management process can become an important part of helping employees understand why their job is important and how it supports organizational strategy.

Chapter 1

Managing Performance

"In the minds of great managers, consistent poor performance is not primarily a matter of weakness, stupidity, disobedience, or disrespect. It is a matter of miscasting." **Marcus Buckingham**

Not all churches embrace the concept of managing employee performance. There may be many reasons for this. The church may not have the resources to create a process, may not know how or may consider it too time consuming and difficult to create a win-win situation.

Some would argue against a formal process for managing performance. Here are some of those arguments:

Time consuming

Churches very often don't bother with managing performance evaluations because it's very time consuming and takes management commitment. The challenge for churches is all of the competing, unpredictable nuances of a church environment. These challenges make it difficult to structure a process, keep with the process and schedule the performance appraisals. For example, a process is created, a PA is scheduled and an unexpected emergency arises with a church member resulting in the need to reschedule the PA. When this happens it is easy to allow it to become less of a priority.

Difficult to create win-win

Inconsistent messages and biases in judgments discourage employees. This is why it's so important to commit to performance management, do it the right way and make sure it's a win-win for everyone. A structure or process that isn't done properly can do more harm than good, so if you commit to doing PAs, invest the time and effort to do it right!

Eight Advantages of Managing Employee Performance

We talked a little about why some organizations don't manage performance. However, the advantages of developing a performance management system are many and well worth the time investment.

1. Performance-based Conversations

A structured performance management process encourages conversations between managers and employees. Some managers are more comfortable having difficult conversations than others. Much of it is personality-driven, but this is a skill everyone can learn. And with training and a little practice we all can become more comfortable having these necessary conversations.

I remember the first time I had to give a performance appraisal; I think I was more scared than the employee. But I was fortunate enough to have a great boss who made sure I had the necessary training before I met with my employee. It ended up being a really positive conversation because I was taught what to do and say.

2. Targeted Staff Development

I'm a huge proponent in developing employees and preparing them for increased responsibility. This is another reason why this process is so important. It naturally incorporates developmental opportunities into the process, which makes an employee's development progression so much easier.

I had an employee who, when I first started working with her, had no computer skills and wasn't even very interested in learning any because she was a little bit older and technology intimidated her. Well, we worked with her, sent her to classes, gave her projects that incorporated her new skills, and I'm so proud of how she not only developed as a more valuable employee but also gained self-confidence in the process.

Encouragement

Employees need constant feedback and encouragement. When employees have the opportunity to discuss their performance at least annually on how well they're doing, it encourages them and provides the motivation to continue to work toward shared goals.

I once had a young employee who had so much potential that I worked very hard to encourage him to develop professionally. I would point out his strengths, coach him through his challenges and provide development opportunities when available. These conversations would literally put him on a high for weeks. You would notice a change in his demeanor and confidence. I made a point of reinforcing the positive, and it really worked for him! He has come a long way, and I'm so proud of him!

3.   Good Performance Rewards

The system inherently identifies the strong performers and monetarily rewards good performance. It really is fun when you sit across the table from high-performing employees and share with them that they received a bigger raise for their efforts. It reinforces positive things and keeps them motivated to work harder.

4.   Underperformers Identified and Eliminated

It's a sad fact, but some people just don't cut the mustard (to succeed; to meet expectations), and this appraisal process forces managers to deal with underperforming employees. This provides an avenue to remove them from the organization.

This is never a pleasant thing to do, but sometimes, underperforming employees need to move on, if for no other reason than for the sake of their coworkers. When employees work hard and see a coworker skimming by and not carrying his or her load, it creates an unhealthy work environment that can affect the rest of the employees, the culture and morale.

It's funny how we managers think we're the only ones who notice underperformers. It's interesting that the few times I've let a poor performer go how employees respond in a positive way. It's as if they knew it all

> **"It's not the people you fire who make your life miserable. It's the people you don't." Dick Grote**

along and didn't think we as management noticed. It's a sad thing when coworkers are more aware of an underperformer than the manager.

5. Documented History of Performance

Another advantage to this process is that it provides a performance trail on every employee. This is very helpful, particularly if new managers come onboard, they can get up to speed quickly on how their employees performed in the past. This also gives management an advantage by having that historical perspective.

6. Succession Planning

I believe everyone has seasons in a professional life. And seasons come and go – even in a church. Church leaders need to constantly look for and develop the next generation of leaders, whether it is in a pastoral capacity or church management.

Not every employee has the motivation or desire to advance within the church, but when the ministry can identify leaders and develop them in a structured format; it's prepared when employees naturally leave employment.

We had a children's director leave within weeks of a huge children's event, and it really threw us for a loop. Fortunately, we had some strong volunteers who helped to bridge the gap, but it took us a few years to get another person up to speed. This kind of sudden transition affects the program, the volunteers and other employees so it's important to constantly think in terms of identifying and developing the next generation of leaders.

Vision Implementation Process

One of the biggest challenges churches face is taking their mission or vision and spreading it throughout the entire organization and helping employees as well as volunteers understand how what they do affects the church's overall goals and strategy. This illustration demonstrates the progression needed to ensure the vision becomes widespread, but it also shows how it ties to each employee's job responsibilities.

Vision Implementation Process

VISION
▽
STRATEGIC PLAN
▽
ORGANIZATIONAL GOALS
▽
DEPARTMENTAL GOALS
▽
EMPLOYEE GOALS
▽
JOB DESCRIPTION
▽
PERFORMANCE APPRAISAL

As you can see, it's really important to understand where the ministry is going. This requires going through a process of developing a mission, a vision and a values statement. This important step is what drives church strategy, which ultimately provides the direction to write church goals.

Once the church develops its goals, delegate them to the appropriate departments and then assign responsibility for completing them to individual employees. This provides the direction for the tasks employees should focus on, which are part of the performance appraisal. Use this simple illustration to visualize the performance management process and demonstrate the importance of tying it all together.

Performance management cycle

Now let's talk a little bit about the performance management cycle.

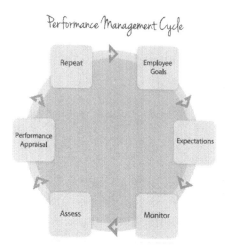

Performance Management Cycle

As you can see from this illustration, the performance management cycle begins with writing employee goals. It's a good idea to make this a project you do WITH the employee and not TO them. Allow employees to ask for clarification or voice concerns with goals so that they understand what's expected and receive assurances that the necessary resources are available for them.

For example, if an employee has a goal to create curriculum for the children's ministry, and it conflicts with some of the daily responsibilities, this is the time the manager should discuss how to cover those other responsibilities to ensure the employee has the time to commit to completing the new goal. This may mean temporarily assigning someone else to the employee's responsibilities or reprioritizing some of what the employee does. This is a great time to use available volunteer resources.

Once the manager and the employee agree to the goals, the manager should clearly explain the expectations, for not only completing the goals but also for the time frame for getting them accomplished. It's so easy to let goals sit on the back burner when an employee is busy, but it's the manager's responsibility to keep the employee focused on completing the goals.

Monitoring the goal process is another manager responsibility. You have to do this to make sure there are no surprises when it's time to assess the employee's performance. The employee is responsible for completing the assigned goals, but the manager is equally responsible for making sure they get it done. This is because the employee's goals should support the completion of the departmental goals the manager is responsible for.

The performance monitoring process helps to provide information for the employee assessment and, ultimately, constructing and writing the performance appraisal. Monitoring performance is an ongoing process that requires following up with the employee to ensure meeting the goals is progressing.

For example, the manager may meet with the employee on a monthly basis and one of the agenda items should be a goal status update. This reminds the employee that their goals will be discussed at least as often as he or she meets with the manager. This step also reminds the manager to discuss goals with the employee. It all ties together, and one step supports the next.

The performance appraisal meeting initiates the goals and expectations for the next cycle and so on.

This isn't rocket science but it does require a process and a commitment from management to see it through. Starting and stopping initiatives discourages employees, but consistency and commitment give employees comfort and encouragement.

Chapter 1 Homework

Meet with your leadership team and discuss the following questions.

- ☐ What is the process to implement our vision?

- ☐ What is our current model for managing performance?

- ☐ How often do we discuss performance with our employees?

- ☐ Do we have a process to develop our employees?

- ☐ What do we do to keep our employees encouraged?

- ☐ Do we reward good performance?

- ☐ Do we do a good job of identifying and removing underperformers?

- ☐ Do we have records in employee files about employee performance?

- ☐ What is our succession plan?

Chapter 2

Setting Goals

"Setting goals is the first step in turning the invisible into the visible." Anthony Robbins

Setting goals is the secret to success by accomplishing those things that move a church forward. Goals provide direction and purpose. If you can see it, you can achieve it. Goals help you see where you're going and how you can get there.

This is particularly important for churches because the nature of ministry is to be constantly dealing with congregational emergencies. This provides church leaders with lots of (very often legitimate) excuses to put goals on the back burner.

Why Set Goals?

Goals provide direction.

Goals provide direction and the necessary steps for completing them. For example, if a church has a strategic goal to open a second campus, it takes many logistical steps to achieve that goal. Breaking goals down into actionable steps allows for movement toward that goal.

Goals tell you how far you've traveled.

Goals tell the organization how far it has traveled and provide a perspective for:

- Where we **were**

- Where we **are**

- Where we're **headed**

When goals are reviewed at least annually, it reminds church leaders about how far they've come. This allows the opportunity to celebrate even seemingly baby steps toward achieving goals.

Goals help to make your overall vision attainable.

God gives churches specific visions and missions, and strategies and goals help to achieve that vision. Goals make a vision attainable by mapping out the steps and process for achieving the vision.

For example, if one of the things God has called your church to is reaching the homeless, strategy and goals can help lay out the systematic steps to achieve that mission. The church leaders do this by identifying the actionable steps needed to get there and assigning the responsibility and resources to someone for completing those action steps.

Goals clarify everyone's role.

Goals help to clarify everyone's role and provide employees with tasks to focus on. This also helps to bridge the gap between what employees do every day and implementing the vision of the church.

For example, having a goal to develop a children's ministry curriculum helps the employees understand what they should spend their time on.

Goals give people something to strive for.

Goals provide an end point, a target, a finish line for employees to strive for. Employees have a great sense of accomplishment when they achieve a goal and can check it off their list. In the example of a project as big as writing a children's ministry curriculum, finishing that goal is a great opportunity to celebrate!

Goals increase performance and when challenging goals are set, research suggests that performance increases between 10 and 25 percent - and sometimes higher.

Goals Need to Be SMART.

SMART is a method of writing goals to ensure they're attainable. The process looks at what the goal is and assigns action steps, accountability and a timeline for completing them.

SMART is an acronym that stands for:

Specific – Is the goal specific enough for clarity?

Measurable – Is there a way to measure the goal? In other words, how do you know you achieved the goal?

Attainable – Is the goal truly attainable? Or is it such an outlandish goal that it looks good on paper but is nearly impossible to complete.

Realistic – Did you write the goal realistically? For example, did you address all the challenges of completing the goal and provide the necessary resources.

Timely – Is there a timeline associated with the goal to ensure a completion date?

> *"If you can't measure and monitor your goals, chances are that your employees will never achieve them and you won't know the difference..." Managing for Dummies*

Taking the time to ask these questions and think through the answers will ensure that goals are truly achievable.

Now let's look at an example goal we can all relate to.

Example goal: **I want to lose weight**.

Now let's ask the SMART goal questions.

- Is it specific? No

- Is it measurable? No

- Is it attainable? Not sure

- Is it realistic? Possibly

- Is it timely? Not sure

Because our answers were so uncertain, we need to look at our goal again and expand it to make it attainable.

Now let's make this goal a SMART goal:

SMART goal: I will lose 15 pounds in three months, starting January 2, by exercising 30 minutes a day, cutting out desserts and snacks and controlling portion sizes.

OK, as you can see, we added dimension to this goal by making it more specific about what we're trying to accomplish and how we plan to achieve it.

Now let's ask those questions again.

Is it specific? – Yes

Losing 15 pounds is very specific. If you had said that you just want to lose "some weight," it's not specific enough to target, but stating how much weight you want to lose gives a clear ending point.

Is it measurable? – Yes

Whether or not you lose the 15 pounds in the three months period is the measure.

Is it attainable? – Yes

Changing your diet and portion sizes makes this goal very attainable. If you didn't specify "how" you were planning to lose the weight, it may not be attainable.

Is it realistic? – Yes

If you had a goal to lose 15 pounds in two weeks, that's not realistic, but thinking through a reasonable approach and timeline makes it achievable.

Is it timely? – Yes

If the goal to start the diet were the third week in November right before the holidays, it's not good timing for the diet. However, since it begins in January, it's very timely. Also allowing enough time to complete the goal makes it attainable.

OK, we can all relate to a personal goal of losing weight, but now let's look at an example of a church goal and how we can develop that using the SMART model.

Example church goal: Increase church membership

OK, let's ask the SMART questions again.

- Is it specific? Not really

- Is it measurable? No

- Is it attainable? Not sure

- Is it realistic? Possibly

- Is it timely? Not defined

Since this goal didn't answer the questions, let's add to the goal and incorporate SMART into it.

Example SMART goal: Increase church membership by 10 percent (400 to 440 members) by 12/31 by adding a Spanish-speaking service

Is it specific? Yes

Determining how much we want to increase membership (400 to 440) makes this goal specific.

Is it measurable? Yes

Determining the percentage increase makes this goal measurable. If we said we want to increase membership without a number attached to it, we have no way to know whether we achieved that goal.

Is it attainable? Yes

This goal is attainable because we know we have had requests for Spanish-speaking services and adding this type of service will meet the needs of our community.

Is it realistic? Yes

This is a realistic goal because there's a high population of Spanish-speaking people in our neighborhood who have asked for Spanish-speaking services so we can confidently say this is a realistic goal.

Is it timely? Yes

We are writing this goal at the beginning of the year so we have ample time to plan a new service and market it to our community.

The key to creating a SMART goal is to have sufficient data to measure. If your church doesn't track church data, maybe it's time to begin. Data answers questions and is invaluable in managing any organization.

Let's look at a few more examples of measurable church goals:

Examples of SMART Goals

- Increase weekly use of volunteers by 20 percent (10 to 12) by 5/1.

- Implement customer service training for 80 percent of employees by 3/20.

- Decrease department monthly supply costs by 10 percent ($1000 to $900) by 12/31.

Writing goals is really about looking at your church and determining those things the church must do to take the ministry to the next level. Base the goals on the church's vision, mission and organizational strategy.

Church managers have a lot to juggle. They have to balance managing the day-to-day operations and doing those things that take the church to the next level. This is where goals come in handy.

Chapter 2 Homework

Discuss these questions with your leadership team and practice writing some church goals.

- ☐ What is our strategy to achieve our mission?

- ☐ How will we know when we get there?

- ☐ Do we have written and measurable goals to get us closer to achieving our vision?

- ☐ Do we know where we were a few years ago as compared to where we are today?

- ☐ Do we have a roadmap for where we are headed?

- ☐ Do employees understand what is expected of them and understand how what they do supports the mission?

- ☐ Let's practice writing a SMART church goal.

- ☐ Let's practice writing a SMART department goal.

- ☐ Let's practice writing a SMART employee goal.

- ☐ Now let's compare the goals to the SMART model? Can we answer yes to the SMART goal questions?

Chapter 3

Creating the PA Form

"Talent is the multiplier. The more energy and attention you invest in it, the greater the yield. The time you spend with your best is, quite simply, your most productive time." Marcus Buckingham

In this chapter we discuss the different dimensions of performance and demonstrate how to tie them to your organizations' values, as well as the employee goals.

Then, we cover rating scales and how to write performance questions for a scale that brings measurable results.

Finally, we talk about how to put it all together, format it and get it ready to use.

Creating a Performance Appraisal Form

We will start by identifying performance measures (dimensions) which will be used to assess the employee.

To create these measures of performance, you need to look at your particular church and identify the desired behaviors or principles that drive the culture of your ministry. So in other words, what behaviors do you expect employees to demonstrate and what principles do you use in the decision-making process?

To do this, look at your organizational values statement. These might be things like customer focus, teamwork, communication or goal achievement or any behavior church leaders expect from employees. For example, if your church understands the importance of creating an atmosphere for everyone to work well together and become team-oriented, then a teamwork dimension is appropriate.

Here are some examples of dimensions and their definitions:

Teamwork: The employee values team interaction and works effectively with others. He or she is a team player and helps encourage and orient new team members. The employee can balance personal effort and project team effort.

Communication: The employee communicates professionally with others and shares thoughts and ideas appropriately. He or she listens to others, asks clarifying questions and controls emotions under pressure.

Customer Focus: The employee understands who the customers are, proactively responds to customer needs and adheres to ministry service standards.

Attendance and Punctuality: The employee shows up for work at the assigned time and provides ample notice when unable to come to work. He or she uses designated time off forms to request time away from job.

Job Knowledge: The employee understands every aspect of the job's tasks and responsibilities and willingly updates job skills. He or she offers assistance to help others improve job skills.

OK, we've identified some of the dimensions (again the behavior we're looking for), and now we want to figure out how to rate or grade that behavior. There are a couple of schools of thought on this and rating scales are typically either a 5-point or 10-point scale.

Many statisticians like to use a 10-point scale because it allows for drilling down into the data to learn more about what drives behavior. For example, when you measure things like customer satisfaction, a 10-point scale might be more appropriate because you're trying to learn why consumers behave in certain ways. But for a performance appraisal form I'm comfortable using a 5-point scale because it's a little easier to construct and do the math.

There are numerous ways to present the questions on a rating scale. Here are a few common ones:

- ➤ Strongly Disagree – Agree - Strongly Agree

- ➤ Never – Sometimes – Always

- ➤ Of no importance – Moderately important – Extremely important

- ➤ Dissatisfied – Satisfied – Extremely satisfied

- ➤ Unsatisfactory – Meets expectations – Outstanding

The way you frame the question determines the scale. For this particular example I used the scale of never-sometimes-always.

Performance appraisal form example

<table>
<tr><td colspan="6" style="text-align:center">ABC Community Church
20XX Performance Appraisal</td></tr>
<tr><td colspan="3">Employee Name:</td><td colspan="3">Department:</td></tr>
<tr><td colspan="6">Please check the box that best describes the frequency of the performance measure.</td></tr>
<tr><td colspan="6">Customer Focus: Employee understands who his/her customers are and proactively responds to customer needs. Employee adheres to ministry service standards with every customer contact.</td></tr>
<tr><td>Employee Self-Assessment</td><td>Never
1</td><td>2</td><td>Sometimes
3</td><td>4</td><td>Always
5</td></tr>
<tr><td>Employee Comments</td><td colspan="5"></td></tr>
<tr><td>Manager Assessment</td><td>Never
1</td><td>2</td><td>Sometimes
3</td><td>4</td><td>Always
5</td></tr>
<tr><td>Manager Comments</td><td colspan="5"></td></tr>
<tr><td colspan="6">Teamwork: Employee values team interactions and works effectively with others. Is a team player and helps encourage and orient new team members. Can balance personal effort with project team effort.</td></tr>
<tr><td>Employee Self-Assessment</td><td>Never
1</td><td>2</td><td>Sometimes
3</td><td>4</td><td>Always
5</td></tr>
<tr><td>Employee Comments</td><td colspan="5"></td></tr>
<tr><td>Manager Assessment</td><td>Never
1</td><td>2</td><td>Sometimes
3</td><td>4</td><td>Always
5</td></tr>
<tr><td>Manager Comments</td><td colspan="5"></td></tr>
<tr><td colspan="6">Job Knowledge: Employee understands every aspect of the job's tasks and responsibilities and willingly updates job skills. Offers assistance to help others improve job skills.</td></tr>
<tr><td>Employee Self-Assessment</td><td>Never
1</td><td>2</td><td>Sometimes
3</td><td>4</td><td>Always
5</td></tr>
<tr><td>Employee Comments</td><td colspan="5"></td></tr>
<tr><td>Manager Assessment</td><td>Never
1</td><td>2</td><td>Sometimes
3</td><td>4</td><td>Always
5</td></tr>
<tr><td>Manager Comments</td><td colspan="5"></td></tr>
<tr><td colspan="6">Communication: Employee communicates professionally with others in writing and shares thoughts and ideas appropriately. Listens to others and asks questions for clarity. Controls emotions under pressure.</td></tr>
</table>

Employee Self-Assessment	Never 1	2	Sometimes 3	4	Always 5
Employee Comments					
Manager Assessment	Never 1	2	Sometimes 3	4	Always 5
Manager Comments					

Attendance and Punctuality: Employee shows up for work at assigned time and provides ample notice when unable to work. Uses designated forms to request time away from work.

Employee Self-Assessment	Never 1	2	Sometimes 3	4	Always 5
Employee Comments					
Manager Assessment	Never 1	2	Sometimes 3	4	Always 5
Manager Comments					

Completion of Goals (refer to goal document):
Goal #1 Develop discipleship program

Employee Self-Assessment	Not Started 1	2	In Process 3	4	Completed
Employee Comments					
Manager Assessment	Not Started 1	2	In Process 3	4	Completed
Manager Comments					

Overall Performance

Employee Self-Assessment	Needs Immediate Improvement 1	2	Meets Require-ments 3	4	Exceeds Expectations
Employee Comments					
Manager Assessment	Needs Immediate Improvement 1	2	Meets Require-ments 3	4	Exceeds Expectations
Manager Comments					

Employee Development Plan (including any continuing education needs).

Employee Signature:	Date:
Manager Signature:	Date

33

In this example form you can see we put the basic demographic information on the top of the form, employee name, what department he or she works in, etc. Then, we take those dimensions and put them on a 5-point scale, using 1 as lowest and 5 as highest rating.

Which means 1 = never, 3 = sometimes and 5 = always.

When I assess my employees' performance, I like to ask them to rate themselves. This is in addition to the managers' assessment, and then I encourage a discussion of each other's perspective. This process can be a little intimidating and scary for employees. This is why the manager needs to explain the process and talk about each of the dimensions. This allows the employees to better understand, learn and grow through the process.

As you can see the form has a section for the employee self-assessment and a section for the manager assessment. Next, there's a section for comments so each can give examples, or expand on a rating if necessary. Document any information used to justify either an extremely high score or an extremely low score on any particular dimension.

The second page of this document incorporates employee goals, which require a change in the wording of the scale. However, it uses the same points system to keep the numbers consistent. Last, there's an overall performance rating. This dimension is important because some employees may score low on certain dimensions because they're in a developmental phase and the manager can use this last dimension to recognize employees who demonstrate overall effort in performing well.

At the bottom of the form there's a place where the employee and manager can comment and document a developmental plan for the employee. For example, if an employee needs to get better at customer service skills, that could be something added to the developmental plan section.

Both the employee and manager should sign the document for the files.

There's an editable copy of this document at http://smartchurchmanagement.com/free-church-forms/.

Chapter 3 Homework

Meet with your leadership team and ask the following questions:

- ☐ What are our core values?

- ☐ How do we want our employees to behave?

- ☐ Who are our customers?

- ☐ What are our customer service standards?

- ☐ Do we have measurable written goals for employees?

- ☐ What is our process to identify developmental opportunities for employees?

- ☐ How can we create a performance appraisal document?

Chapter 4

PA Process

"Careers are developed one conversation at a time – over time." Beverly Kaye – Julie Giulioni

In this chapter we talk about setting and communicating performance expectations and their importance. Then, we discuss the significance of continually assessing an employee's performance. This is, for the most part, developing a process that pays attention to what they're doing, what they're doing well and what they could do a little differently or in a better way.

All employees want to know whether they're doing a good job. Formal performance evaluations **force** managers to communicate performance results – both good and bad – to employees.

Setting expectations for employees is one of the most important steps in managing performance. It's not fair to assess people on something they didn't know was expected or that they didn't have a clear understanding of.

This is also an area that many supervisors could do a better job in, but they're so busy, they don't always **think** about those things that are important to employees. I've had countless managers come to me frustrated about an employee who wasn't performing up to their expectations, and the first question I always ask is, "Did you clearly say what you wanted them to do, and did they understand the expectation?" If the answer to either of those questions is no, then, I would argue it's not the employee who's at fault but the manager!

For example, I had a manager tell an employee to "reorganize the warehouse." There was never a timeline given for completing the project, and the manager never followed up to see what the progress was on the directive. After a six-month period the manager remembered giving the directive and was upset the employee didn't do it. In this example, they were both to blame.

Because the manager didn't follow up with the employee, the employee didn't think the manager really meant the directive, and the manager not following up reinforced that perception.

So what things are important for managers to discuss with employees?

Department and Employee Goals

Discuss department and employee goals on a regular basis. Research suggests that the more you keep a goal in the forefront the more likely it's achievable. Think of the illustration of someone needing to lose weight and putting a picture on the refrigerator as a constant reminder.

If you write the goals at the beginning of the year and then file them in some cabinet, the less likely they're achievable. Keep goal status a standing agenda item for manager/employee update meetings.

Job Descriptions

Job descriptions are another source of performance expectations. Review job descriptions at least once a year and incorporate employee goals into job tasks. Also, update the job description document so you can remove tasks that were important a few years ago, but no longer add value.

Most employees want to perform well and feel reassured when they can look at a document and know exactly how they should spend their time. For example, I had an employee whose job was to track daily job tasks for the custodial department to gather information for a project we were working on. The project was

> *"There is nothing so useless as doing efficiently that which should not be done at all."*
> *Peter F. Drucker*

long finished, and I learned she was diligently continuing to track the daily job tasks because I didn't tell her to stop. We discovered this by reviewing her job description, which is why it's so important to know exactly how employees spend their time.

Continuous Communication/Coaching

I believe there's never too much communication with employees, and it's an important responsibility of every supervisor and manager. Employees crave feedback and should hear when they're doing things right and know of the times they could perform better.

For example, I worked with a manager who would tell me how rude her employee was

> *It's not fair to assess people on something they didn't know was expected or that they didn't have a clear understanding of.*

to customers on the phone but **wasn't comfortable** coaching her employee on a better way to respond to customers. I consider this the manager's problem more than the employee's because the employee may not even know how he or she comes across on the phone. It's the manager's responsibility to help them with self-awareness.

Documenting these seemingly insignificant conversations is one of the best ways to gather data for performance appraisal time. It's so easy to forget these day-in and day-out conversations, so here are a few tips:

Tip

✓ Whenever you recognize a problem with your employees' performance, mention it to them, make a note of it and drop it in their files.

✓ Whenever your employees do something great, mention it to them, <u>make a note</u> and drop it in their files.

Another tool I use is what I call a simple note-taking log. I create a document on each employee. You can do this on a page in the back of your planner if you're a Franklin Planner addict, or you can use an Excel spreadsheet or just keep a note on your phone or Blackberry. The tool you use doesn't matter as much as consistently recording conversations with the employee.

Here's an example of what a log might look like. Keep in mind you're not writing a dissertation; you're merely putting enough information down to trigger a memory for you. The goal is to make the process quick and efficient, not to burden you with another chore. The following examples should give you an idea of some of the things you can document. Remember that you want to capture both positive and negative behavior. Taking the time to do this will prove invaluable when you sit down to fill in the performance appraisal form and try to objectively evaluate an employee for an entire rating period.

Note-Taking Log Example

Name	Date	Incident Description	Persons Involved	Action Taken
Sue Smith	Jan 3	Sue went above and beyond by preparing a presentation without being told.	Sue Smith	Orally acknowledged and thanked Sue for taking care of project independently.
	Feb 9	Sue was 45 minutes late for work.	Sue	Orally reminded Sue of tardy policy.
	April 6	Quarterly report to the Board had three typos.	Sue	Orally pointed out typos and coached Sue on proofing.
	June 12	Sue worked late voluntarily to finish report for Jim.	Sue	Orally thanked Sue.

So Why Do Performance Appraisals?

Performance appraisals are a tool used to reinforce positive behaviors and course-correct where needed. It's so easy for any of us to veer off track if there isn't a constant reminder of priorities and the desired direction to follow, which is why these conversations are so important. Also there are times when employees just need help prioritizing job tasks. I've had employees that, when you give them directions to do something, they keep doing it until you tell them to stop. If additional tasks are assigned to the employee, this results in wasted time and resources, and causes an employee a lot of undue confusion and stress.

> *"If you don't monitor desired performance, you won't achieve desired performance. Don't leave achieving your goals to chance; develop systems to monitor progress and ensure that your goals are achieved...." – Managing for Dummies*

When we're trudging through the day-to-day responsibilities, we have the tendency to lose sight of the big picture and recognize how much we're actually accomplishing. This is a time to reflect and celebrate accomplishments over the course of the past 12 months and thank employees for all they do which is critical to keeping them encouraged and engaged with the organization.

Performance appraisals need to be fair, relevant and complete!

Fair

The appraisal needs to be fair and unbiased. This is challenging because sometimes we honestly don't like some of the employees who work for us. Not all managers will admit this, but it is so true! But that bias must not influence the appraisal. We'll pursue this more when we discuss rater errors.

To be fair, you have to observe all employees and document behavior in the same way in terms of frequency, type of language used, harshness of judgment and interim feedback.

Ask yourself:

- ✓ Would you have written the same notation on a different employee?

- ✓ Did you overemphasize a single event?

It is also important to give feedback as soon as you see a problem so you're giving the employee a chance to improve.

Relevant

The appraisal needs to be relevant to the entire evaluation period and to the performance of the job and the specific standards and/or expectations that you and the employee have established.

To make the appraisal relevant, refer to internal policies, standards and employee goals (i.e., service standards, attendance policy, etc.). Focus on behavior and results. Ask the question, did the employees finish their goals; did they contribute to the mission of the church?

Complete

Finish writing the appraisal with documented information and completed goals. Complete means monitoring and documenting employee performance should tell a **complete** story about the employee for the entire rating period. It's also essential to note unusual circumstances that may affect the performance and include accomplishments that indicate strong performance. Remember to make sure you document both positive and negative observations.

You should periodically review your observations so a third party, who might review the information, gets an accurate picture of the employee's performance.

OK, let's now talk a little bit about performance rater errors. A rater error is defined as:

"A barrier to the accuracy and credibility of performance measures is posed by a number of rater errors, perceptual biases and other sources of distortion in performance ratings." – Human Resource Strategy

There are five common rater errors that managers make when assessing employee performance. As we go through each of these, see if you recognize any of these tendencies in yourself. I was really surprised at the accuracy of some of these for me personally, and they helped me a lot when I became familiar with them.

Halo Effect

A rater's overall positive or negative impression of an individual employee leads to rating him or her the same across all rating dimensions. Think of that favorite employee that you might golf with or that problem employee you might have a personality conflict with and ask yourself, "Am I being objective with this assessment?"

Leniency Error

This is a rater's tendency to rate all employees at the positive end of the scale (positive leniency) or at the low end of the scale (negative leniency). Sometimes emotions drive how we rate an employee so it isn't objective.

Central Tendency Error

Central tendency error is the raters' tendency to avoid making **extreme** judgments of employee performance, resulting in rating all employees in the middle part of a scale. This can happen either when a manager isn't comfortable with conflict and avoids low marks to avoid dealing with a behavioral issue or when a manager intentionally forces all employees to the middle of the scale.

Recency Errors

Recency error is the raters' tendency to allow more recent incidents (either effective or ineffective) of employee behavior to carry too much weight in the evaluation of performance over an entire rating period. This can be extreme on both ends of the spectrum. For example, either an employee just finished a major project successfully, or an employee may have had a negative incident right before the performance appraisal process, and it's at the forefront of the manager's thoughts. A manager can avoid these pitfalls if he or she keeps accurate, ongoing records of performance throughout the year. Then, he or she can refer to notes during appraisal time to help remain objective.

First Impression Error

First impression error is a rater's tendencies to let first impressions of employee performance carry too much weight when evaluating performance over an entire rating period. For example, if you hire a new employee who starts off strong, but may waver over the course of a year and you base their rating on your first impression of their performance.

Similar-to-me Error

This is a rater's tendency to show bias in performance evaluation toward those employees seen as similar to the raters themselves. For example, it's easier for all of us to relate to people who have similar social styles, but being relatable should not affect a performance rating.

There are a couple of things to keep in mind when preparing for the PA:

- Decide what information to include and not to include in the final appraisal form. Take this information from the entire rating period. Remember the note-taking log we talked about? This is the time to pull that out and refresh your memory.

- Focus on pulling the kind of information that might show some patterns in behavior for an entire period. As you look at the information, watch for patterns of both positive and not so positive behavior.

- A performance appraisal conversation should never be the first time you tell an employee of a performance issue. Because you have communicated with and coached the employee the entire period, none of this is new information for them, and there should be no surprises. It's not fair to surprise an employee with something they may not even know they did wrong.

- It's vital to block out time on your calendar so you can focus on this project. I always tell managers to allow at least one hour for each employee to make sure they give the necessary time to ensure the appraisal is truly **fair**, **relevant** and **complete**.

- Organize the material and all the information you gathered over the performance period and review it to make sure it's clear in your mind so you can remember the details during your conversation with the employee.

Here's how to prepare for the performance appraisal conversation.

- ✓ When you schedule the performance appraisal, make it for an appropriate time and neutral place (if possible). For example, you probably don't want to do an appraisal on a day there are a lot of other stressful events going on, and you don't want to do it in your office. Use a conference room, which is a more neutral place that allows the employee to be a bit more relaxed.

- ✓ Make sure your meeting time is free of interruptions. Once you get in a good rhythm with the employee, you don't want someone inadvertently interrupting and affecting the conversation.

✓ Go into the meeting prepared with specific examples of effective and ineffective performance to share with the employee. Keep in mind that you have kept notes, but you may need to remind the employee of some of the conversations you've had.

Now it's time to have the conversation.

✓ It's always good to ease into the conversation by stating the purpose of appraisal and explaining the process of the discussion. For example, you could say something like this.

"Tim, I will be reviewing this performance appraisal with you. I know you had a chance to do a self-assessment so today we'll discuss each of the dimensions and talk about both of our perceptions of your performance. We will then review your goals and together come up with a developmental plan for next year. Do you have any questions?"

This preliminary conversation helps get both you and the employee on the same page.

✓ Review the appraisal with the employee and explain any parts of the form he or she may not understand, especially if this is the first time going through a process like this. For example, explain the rating scale and the dimension definitions.

✓ As you talk with the employee, make sure you probe for additional information, misunderstandings or views that may differ from yours. Watch body language and try to keep a pulse on what he or she is thinking. You want the employee to feel comfortable enough to ask clarifying questions and give honest responses.

✓ Once you get through the entire document, summarize the performance discussion and talk about next steps. For example, if you have identified a developmental goal, talk about how to find information on a particular class and walk the employee through the process of moving forward.

✓ Discuss goals and a development plan and give the employee the opportunity to ask questions or voice concerns.

✓ Ask the employee to sign the appraisal form. On rare occasions an employee will say no and refuse to sign the form but explain that the signature is merely acknowledgement of the conversation and not necessarily an agreement with it. At that point you can discuss what grievance options there are. This is a rare incident, but it does happen occasionally.

✓ Remember the outcome of this process is only as good as management's commitment to it. Managers must commit significant amounts of time on a regular basis to performance management to be effective. This is how you manage work.

Know that a lack of clear performance expectations and detailed performance feedback are major sources of stress for employees so anything a manager can do by communicating can help alleviate that stress.

We mentioned this earlier, but this is a good time to make sure the employee's job description reflects what he or she is actually doing and includes previously set goals. Review the document and remove responsibilities that are no longer necessary and add those tasks that support goal completion.

Chapter 4 Homework

Meet with your management team, and as a group discuss these questions. Encourage honesty and try to learn from one another.

- ☐ Does your department write employee goals?

- ☐ When was the last time anyone updated employee job descriptions?

- ☐ How often do you meet with your employees to discuss performance?

- ☐ When is the last time you coached your employee to better performance?

- ☐ Do you keep a log of conversations that you have with your employees?

- ☐ Do you have employees that you like better than others?

- ☐ Do you think you can assess all employees without bias?

- ☐ If you answer no, why not?

Chapter 5

Scoring and Raises

"Lack of salary increase does create the belief that you're underpaid, or certainly that you could do better elsewhere." Bill Coleman

In this chapter we'll cover budgeting for raises, how to score your performance appraisal and how to tie the scores to raise distribution. This process is an objective way to make sure your best performers are getting a higher percentage of the raise dollars.

OK, let's look at the document again and see the dimension scores. When you rate employees, they receive a score based on the rating you determined. To score the employee, do the math on all the ratings to get an average score. Let's look at an example:

Let's say that on dimension 1 there was a score of three, dimension 2 a score of three, dimension 3 a score of four, and so on.

This is what that might look like.

Dimension 1	Score = 3
Dimension 2	Score = 3
Dimension 3	Score = 4
Dimension 4	Score = 3
Dimension 5	Score = 5
Dimension 6	Score = 3
Dimension 7	Score = 4
	Total = **25**

What you want to do is total the scores. In this particular example if you add up the scores you get a total score of 25 out of a possible 35 (7x5).

Total Score = 25 out of possible 35

Now if you take that score of 25 and divide it by 7 (the number of dimensions) you get an average score of 3.5

Average score = 25/7 = **3.5**

Now you want to do this on all of your employees and come up with a list of average scores.

OK, we have the scores but how do you tie those scores to raises?

Let's go through an example. Let's say for the sake of easy math that you have:

☐ 11 employees each making $10/hour.

☐ Let's also say:

- The church board approved a budgeted 3.5 percent this year for raises. That 3.5 percent equals a pool of raise dollars of $8,008.

- You get this dollar amount by taking the salaries of those 11 employees and multiplying it by 3.5 percent (.035x$228,800).

- The $228,800 comes from 11 (employees) x 2080 (hours) x 10 (dollars an hour) or 11 x 2080 x 10 = a salary budget for those employees of $228,800.

☐ Now let's also say you determined that average scores (3.0) will receive a 3.5 percent increase and those scoring below average will receive less, those scoring above will receive more.

Now let's look at what this might look like:

Average Employee Scores and Percentage Increase

Emp.	Avg. Score	% Increase	Increase hour	Increase	Bud.	Diff.
A	3	3.5%	$10x.035=$.35	$728		
B	4	4%	$10x.04=$.40	$832		
C	3	3.5%	$10x.035=$.35	$728		
D	2	2%	$10x.02=$.20	$416		
E	3	3.5%	$10x.035=$.35	$728		
F	3.5	3.5%	$10x.035=$.35	$728		
G	2.5	2%	$10x.02=$.20	$416		
H	4	4%	$10x.04=$.40	$832		
I	4.5	4.5%	$10x.45=$.45	$936		
J	4.5	4.5%	$10x.45=$.45	$936		
K	3.5	3.5%	$10x.035=$.35	$728		
Avg. Score	3.4		Total Raises	$8,008	$8,008	$ -0-

As you can see there are 11 employees listed, A, B, C, etc. The next column shows their average scores as well as an overall average score for all employees of 3.4 (pretty good).

Now, in the next column you can see the percentage increase awarded to each employee based on your predetermined criteria. Some received as low as a 2 percent increase and the higher performers received as high as 4.5 percent increase. This translates into a raise of $416 (.20 X 2080) for the poor performers but more than twice as much, $936 (.45 X 2080) for the higher-performing employees. If you total what all of these increases add up to, you see at the bottom that these pay increases will cost the church $8,008, which ends up being the budgeted amount or $8,008.

Keep in mind this is an oversimplified example to demonstrate how to do this. Obviously, when there are dozens or even hundreds of employees, this scenario would look much different.

Larger organizations allocate the raise percentage to the individual department and allow managers to award raises specifically to their own area.

Another important thing to remember is good communication when you tell employees about their raises. The higher performers should know they received a higher percentage because of good performance, but the lower performers should know they received less because of their performance scores.

This process should result positively for the good performers and a wakeup call for the underperformers. Employees who receive a less than average raise, need to have a clear understanding about why. It's not an enjoyable conversation, but the organization owes honesty to the employee.

It is also common to have a three-strike rule when it comes to performance appraisals. If the employee consistently scores below average, the manager should determine if the employee needs additional training or if the employee is in the wrong job. Leadership should determine if they need to train, transfer or terminate the employee if the performance does not improve. Allowing an employee to stay in a job that is not a good fit is not fair to the employee or the organization.

Finally, it doesn't matter how high the percentage of raise, most employees don't think it's enough. We all think we're worth more than we get paid. That's just something you need to know and not get overly concerned about. Statistics show most people don't think they're paid what they're worth, and there's a perception that organizations have unlimited resources for salaries. We all know that's not true!

Chapter 5 Homework

Meet with your leadership team and discuss the following:

- ☐ What percentage do we budget for raises?

- ☐ How do we determine that percentage?

- ☐ What percentage increase will our average performers receive?

- ☐ What percentage increase will high performers receive?

- ☐ What percentage increase will our underperformers receive?

- ☐ Do we believe that a poor performer should not get a raise?

- ☐ How will we communicate raise information with our employees?

Chapter 6 Employee Engagement

"An engaged employee is one who is fully involved in and enthusiastic about their work and will act in a way that furthers their organization's interest." – Wikipedia

Successful organizations understand the importance of engaged employees. Employees need to feel as if they do meaningful work and what they do makes a difference.

People who work for a ministry feel as if they're fulfilling a calling. When church employees engage with the organization, their call reaches a whole new level. They put their hearts and souls into their jobs and have the energy and excitement to give more than is required of them.

When employees do not engage, it can have a negative impact on the work environment and the customer experience. For churches that's other employees, volunteers and church members.

According to Scarlett Surveys, 31 percent of employees are disengaged, and 4 percent of those disengaged employees are hostile. If these survey results are correct, what can organizations do to improve employee engagement levels?

Organizations with strong employee engagement have figured out how to create a culture that fosters engaged employees. They understand the role of leadership in communicating, developing and rewarding employees.

So what are some ways to create an employee engagement culture?

Inspiring Vision

Cultures with high employee engagement have a defined and well-communicated vision. This is another reason to go through a visioning process, if you haven't done so already.

Those in church leadership are responsible for communicating the vision and keeping it in front of the employees. Employees should know the church vision, articulate it and understand why it does what it does. Employees who emotionally attach to the vision believe in what they do and are committed and loyal to the organization.

Consistent Communication

Good communication is one of the most important things a church can do to foster employee engagement. Employees spend a good portion of their lives at work and have an interest in what's going on within the organization. They want to know how the church is doing financially, how ministry goals are being accomplished and how what they do contributes to achieving overall church objectives.

For example, what is it that the receptionist does that contributes to the mission of the church? There can never be too much communication to reinforce how what an employee does impacts fulfilling the mission!

Supervisor Interaction

There's a lot of research that suggests that employees leave organizations because of their direct supervisor. The engagement of employees ties directly to the supervisor's **leadership abilities**. This includes how he or she shares information, how employees perceive equity with each other and how well a supervisor demonstrates care for employees as individuals.

> *Employees want to know they're valued as people.*

Employees want to know they're valued as people. Church leaders need to tend to the employee flock as much as (if not more than) the congregation because of the call and the intense spiritual battle that comes with being a church employee.

Employee Development

Most employees welcome the opportunity to develop and grow professionally. They need the chance to grow in their jobs and within the organization. You can do this by having a defined developmental plan for each employee. (Remember we put that in the PA form.) Church managers should constantly **coach** their employees to fine-tune skills and develop new ones.

Team Environment

Strong employee engagement is dependent on how well employees get along, interact with each other and participate in a team environment. Developing a strong church staff team can help foster engaged employees. You should have a no tolerance policy for strife and discord. Employees need to feel as if they belong to a community, a team and a family. Coworkers are the only family some employees have so maintaining a work environment where all employees feel part of a team, and work well together, is very important.

Culture of Trust

Employees need to trust each other as well as church leadership. Employees are constantly watching leadership to see how their decisions affect the church's strategic direction and if their behavior reflects what they say. In a lot of ways managing employees is similar to raising kids. They don't do what you say they do what you do. People are always observing church leaders even in their private lives – no double standards allowed.

Clear Expectations

Employees need to know what you expect of them (see chapter 4). You can do this by assigning specific goals as well as providing the training, tools and resources needed to perform their job. You also have to hold employees accountable for achieving their goals through a structured performance management process.

Reward and Recognition

Employees need to feel validated and acknowledged as an intrinsic part of the organization. Strong church leadership demonstrates how much it cares for employees and shows recognition for employee efforts. Integrate rewards and recognition into the way you manage employees on a day-to-day basis.

Employee Satisfaction

Employees need to feel as if they're part of the process, that their thoughts and ideas matter and that they have a voice in how they perform the work. They're on the front line and know best about how to do their jobs. Actively soliciting employee feedback and incorporating employee thoughts and ideas into how the church operates is a very effective way to engage employees.

Competitive Pay and Benefits

While pay and benefits are not the key indicators of employee engagement, offering competitive compensation, benefits and reasonable working conditions is a strategy for strong employee engagement. People don't work for a church because of the money, but they do deserve comparable pay. Developing a culture that supports employee engagement can have a positive effect on the employee and the church's ability to achieve its mission and vision.

Church leaders sometimes make the mistake of taking for granted a calling an employee has and neglects the very things that enhance the calling. Make it a priority to proactively look for ways to engage employees.

Chapter 6 Homework

Meet with your leadership team and ask the following questions:

- ☐ Are our employees engaged with our organization?

- ☐ Are any employees not engaged?

- ☐ Can we attribute that disengagement to our leadership model?

- ☐ How often do we talk about our mission and vision with employees?

- ☐ How do we make sure we communicate clearly and effectively with our staff?

- ☐ How good a job do our supervisors do in interacting with employees?

- ☐ Do we have a process to track and develop our employees?

- ☐ What is our succession plan?

- ☐ How well do our employees work together?

- ☐ Do our employees trust us, and each other?

- ☐ How good a job do we do articulating expectations for employees?

- ☐ How would employees grade our rewards and recognition of them?

- [ ] Do our employees enjoy working here, or do they stay here for the sake of the calling?

- [ ] How competitive are our pay and benefits as compared to other organizations?

Parting Words

Managing church operations requires the ability to achieve objectives by managing and overseeing the day-to-day performance of employees and volunteers.

Almost anyone who has managed people or had someone manage him or her has experienced the sometimes stressful, time-consuming process of managing employee performance. However, a well-designed and consistently managed performance management process is rewarding for both the employee as well as the manager. There's nothing sweeter to an employee's ear than hearing the words "good job," and there's nothing more fulfilling for a manager than to watch an employee develop and grow professionally!

I hope this book helps you and your church as you strive to manage the employees whom God has provided to you as a partner to achieve your mission!

Also, I hope these sample documents provide your organization with a jumpstart in the process of developing your own tools to help you manage employee performance.

You may access editable copies of the PA form at http://smartchurchmanagement.com/free-church-forms/. Please feel free to download copies and modify them for your church.

If you have any thoughts or feedback about this book, please comment at http://smartchurchmanagement.com/contact/. Your feedback will help me make improvements to this book.

If I can offer further support, I would love to help you think through the steps of creating a culture of strong employee performance.

God bless you in all you do!

Patricia

Patricia Lotich
Smart Church Management
patricia@smartchurchmanagement.com

Websites:
SmartChurchManagement.com
ThrivingSmallBusiness.com

About the Author

Patricia Lotich is the founder of Smart Church Management and Thriving Small Business. As a business performance consultant Patricia helps organizations manage their resources of people, time and money.

Patricia is the author of two books – both are available on Amazon:
Smart Church Management: A Quality Approach to Church Administration

Smart Volunteer Management: A Volunteer Coordinator's Handbook for Engaging, Motivating and Developing Volunteers

She also writes for the National Association of Church Business Administration (NACBA), Yahoo Small Business Advisor, and Technorati and was a contributing author for American Express Open Forum.

Patricia Lotich has an MBA and is a Certified Manager of Quality and Organizational Excellence through the American Society for Quality. She has 10 years of business administration and church operations experience and has a driving passion to help churches fulfill their call by managing the resources God gave them – people, time and money.

Patricia became a Christian as an adult and has committed herself to using her business experience and gifts to help the local church.

About SCM

Smart Church Management (SCM) is a church operations and management consulting company that offers services to help the local church, small businesses and nonprofit organizations develop systems and processes to support business development and growth.

Whether the system is to manage and budget limited resources; recruit, train and schedule volunteers; or the process of hiring, training and developing employees, SCM strives to help organizations manage their day-to-day operations.

If you would like to schedule a free 30-minute consultation and learn how Smart Church Management can help your organization, please contact SCM at info@smartchurchmanagement.com.

Phone: 314-229-4147

Additional References

Blanchard, K. and Ridge, G., *Helping People Win at Work*, Polvera Publishing and Garry Ridge, 2009.

Evans, J.R. and Lindsay, W.M., *The Management and Control of Quality*, South-Western, a division of Thomson   Learning, 2002.

Grote, D. *The Complete Guide to Performance Appraisal*, American Management Association, 1996.

LaFasto, F. and Larson, C., *When Teams Work Best*, Sage Publications, 2001.

Nelson, B. and Economy, P., *Managing for Dummies*, Wiley Publishing, Inc., 2003.

Maxwell, J.C., *The 21 Irrefutable Laws of Leadership*, Maxwell Motivation, Inc., 1998.

Warren, R., *The Purpose Driven Church*, Zondervan Publishing House, 1995.

Westcott, R.T., *The Certified Manager of Quality/Organizational Excellence*, American Society for Quality, Quality Press, Milwaukee, Wisconsin 53203, 2006.

Made in the USA
Lexington, KY
18 January 2017